THE Doaks of Montana

by Monty Ward

illustrated by Tim Jones

PEARSON

Scott
Foresman

Editorial Offices: Glenview, Illinois • Parsippany, New Jersey • New York, New York
Sales Offices: Needham, Massachusetts • Duluth, Georgia • Glenview, Illinois
Coppell, Texas • Ontario, California • Mesa, Arizona

Ellie Doak usually had no trouble with her aim. She was twelve years old and had been hunting rabbits for years. She was the best hunter in a household that included four boys, better even than her older brother, Clark. Her family had come to depend on the meat she put on their table. Ellie liked romping alone under the big Montana sky. It helped her to think and sort out her troubles. Today, however, she couldn't shake her worries, and her aim was suffering.

Ellie had seen plenty of rabbits dart through the grass today. But when she raised her gun to take a shot, she missed every time. The rabbits were too fast for her. More likely, she was too slow for them. In fact, she had been moving slowly all afternoon, uneasy at the thought of returning home. She knew her father and his new wife would be back by the time she got there.

It had been a little more than a year since Ellie's mother, Ruby, died of pneumonia during the harshest winter any of them had ever known. Ellie would never forget it. Snow was piled high around their cabin, and more kept coming. It grew colder every week. Ruby developed a cough. It quickly grew worse and settled in her lungs. In March, it finally took her.

When Henry Doak decided to remarry, he gathered his children together and told them what he expected. First, they were to obey their new stepmother. Her name was Patience. She wouldn't replace their mother; he knew that. But he did expect them to be kind to her. He planned to take the wagon into town. He would be back in three days with Patience.

What would Patience be like? Ellie wondered about that for the hundredth time that day. How would Patience manage a cabin full of rowdy boys? Would she expect Ellie, who was as strong as any of her brothers, to do only women's work? Ellie's mother had never insisted on that.

The Doaks had always shared the work equally. Ellie's brothers took turns doing the dishes. And no one could round up cattle faster than Ellie—as long as she didn't have to ride sidesaddle like the other girls. Sometimes visitors were a little shocked by Ellie's rowdy ways.

Once, in a fit of frustration, she cut her long skirt up the middle. She stitched the two pieces together to make a pair of bloomers. Her mother had understood. It was much easier to hunt, cut hay, or do any other outdoor chore in bloomers than in a skirt that tangled around your legs. Now she only wore skirts indoors.

Ruby didn't care what visitors thought of her daughter. She was pleased that Ellie had a mind of her own. She was quick and sensible—good things for any girl living in wild Montana to be. But what would Patience think of Ellie?

Ellie took a few deep breaths to try and calm her fears. It would be nice, she thought, to fix her father a wedding dinner of rabbit stew. Would this new woman care for the taste of rabbit? It was a Doak family favorite.

"She has to like it," Ellie said out loud. "She just has to."

Just then, a flicker in the grass caught Ellie's eye. There was her rabbit! She aimed, shot, and finally hit her mark. He was a big speckled one. She picked up the rabbit, shouldered her gun, and turned to head home.

When Ellie stepped through the cabin door, clutching the rabbit by its hind legs, the first thing that caught her eye was the new bonnet sitting on the table. She felt her heart skip a beat. It belonged to Patience.

"Ellie," her father approached her and ushered her further into the house, "I'd like you to meet Patience."

It took a minute for Ellie's eyes to adjust to the dimness in the cabin. It had only three small windows. The furnishings were sparse. Bunks and shelves lined two of the walls. Henry Doak had made them from wood pried off the wagon that had carried the family to Montana. The Doaks, like most settlers, made do with what they had.

"We'll get things figured out," was always Ruby's cheerful response when faced with a new challenge. When Clark was born, he needed a cradle. Ruby used a large wooden bowl, curved almost to the bottom. Ever since, all of the Doak babies spent their first few months rocking in that bowl.

They had brought just one piece of fine furniture with them. It was a small chest that had belonged to Ruby's mother. Ruby had used it to store a few precious things. Among them were the dress she was married in, letters from home, and her diary.

Now, the chest was Ellie's. In it, Ellie had carefully stashed a picture of her mother. It had been taken years ago on Ruby's wedding day. Ellie spent many evenings sorting the letters and refolding her mother's dress. She always tucked the picture carefully inside before closing the chest.

The chest wasn't just for storage, though. It was also a seat. Ellie dragged it to the table at mealtime and pushed it back to the wall when she was through. She liked being close to her mother's things. Sitting on the chest, she felt protected.

Ellie's eyes met her father's for a moment and then turned to the wall. There was Patience, studying her closely. Her eyebrows were arched. Her lips were set in a narrow line, and Ellie wondered if she ever smiled. Her hands lay folded in her lap, and she was sitting very straight. Then Ellie noticed what seat Patience had chosen: the chest.

"Hello, Ellie," said Patience. Her tone was formal.

Get off! thought Ellie. *That's Ma's chest.*

The folds of Patience's skirt draped over the edges of the chest. They just about made the whole thing disappear. Suddenly, Ellie felt like lunging at this woman with her fine clothes. She wanted to knock her off the chest. It took all her strength to stand still.

"Ellie!" said her father sternly. "Patience spoke to you." Ellie glanced at him quickly.

Traitor, she thought. *Why did you bring her here?*

She said nothing, but nodded curtly to Patience before turning toward the door.

"I brought you this," she said. She slung the rabbit on the table and ran out.

Patience was polite about the rabbit stew at supper. But Ellie noticed she hadn't eaten much. Patience spent the meal trying to make conversation with the children. No one seemed to be in the talking mood. They had eaten in silence, swatting at the mosquitoes and flies that buzzed through the open door. Ellie's brother Cyrus lit a nub of dried buffalo dung to try and keep the bugs away. All it did was make the cabin smoky.

"Ellie, I want you to help Patience clean up," said her father, shoving away from the table when supper was over. "The boys will help me with the chores in the barn."

Ellie glared at her father. It was her turn for barn duty. Why was he ordering her to stay inside? She didn't dare argue with him, though. He had already spoken to her once that evening about her sour behavior.

"Give Patience a chance!" he hissed at Ellie when Patience had stepped out. "And for goodness sake, put on a dress!"

Ellie and Patience were working in silence, dishes clattering in the metal tub, when Patience got that chance. Neither of them heard the skunk as it shuffled through the open door of the cabin. It ambled over to the table and sniffed near Ellie's feet.

Patience suddenly noticed it. She gasped and swirled around. Her skirt brushed the side of the skunk. Terrified, it darted under Ellie's skirt and sprayed every bit of stink it had. Ellie screamed. The skunk bolted out the door just as five-year-old Walter came in.

The two plowed into each other. Walter tripped over the creature and tumbled headfirst into the sharp edge of the table. He burst into tears. Blood dribbled down his nose from a gash in his forehead.

To Ellie's surprise, Patience jumped into action, just as Ruby would have. She ordered Ellie to go outside, fill some buckets with water, and take off her smelly clothes. Then Patience scooped Walter up and set him on her lap. She swabbed his wound with a clean, wet rag. After that, she grabbed a bar of lye soap and went to find Ellie.

Both of them stank. Their hair smelled like skunk. Their skin smelled like skunk. They could taste the skunk on their tongues. The water in the buckets was icy cold. They scrubbed themselves pink. Then they wrapped up in blankets and headed back to the cabin. Ellie was glad to have had company through the ordeal. Maybe having a stepmother wouldn't be so bad after all.

The next morning, Patience was up and dressed before anyone else. She had on a fresh linen skirt and blouse. She laid out one of her skirts at the foot of Ellie's bed. She wasn't sure if the girl had another of her own to wear, and Patience was happy to share what she had.

When Ellie woke, she saw the skirt. Was it meant as a peace offering? Ellie touched the fabric. It was finely woven wool and linen with red stripes on a brown background. The colors suited Ellie. But she wasn't ready for peace yet. Instead, she pulled on her old bloomers and slipped out to tend to her morning chores.

School was in session for the summer, but there was still work around the Doak place to do. Sawing, splitting, and stacking wood was a job that lasted all summer. The children had stopped complaining about it after their mother had died. The winter she caught pneumonia, there hadn't been quite enough wood to keep them all warm.

Ellie couldn't help but blame herself for her mother's sickness. She had been lazy about her wood chores the summer before. She was always looking for a way to get out of them. Cyrus had done the same.

Now, the two of them had teamed up. They had a quiet competition going to see how much wood they could chop each week. Their goal was to beat the amount from the week before. They became fast at using the axe.

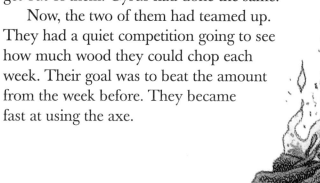

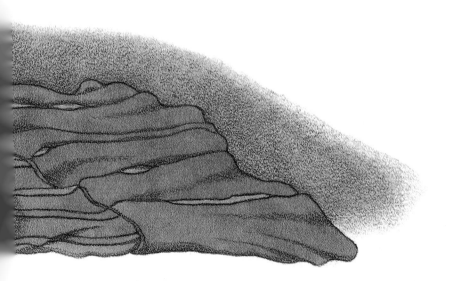

Summer passed quickly. In her mind Ellie had reached a truce with Patience. It helped that her brothers liked their stepmother. Patience was a hard worker, just as their mother had been. Patience appreciated the work the Doak children did too, and she said so.

Ellie found herself looking through her mother's chest less often these days. But on the evenings when she did, Patience would sit by her side and ask about Ruby.

"She was beautiful," Patience said, studying Ruby's picture. "You look like her."

Ellie blushed. No one had ever noticed her looks before. She never really thought about them herself. It pleased her to be likened to her mother.

Fall set in. The evenings were cooler. Her father and Clark hitched up the wagon for the three-day trip to town to get supplies for the winter.

The night they left, it was unusually cold. Ellie added extra wood to the fire. The heat felt good, and it made them sleepy.

The younger boys went to sleep early. Ellie felt content when she finally climbed into bed. The root cellar, where the family stored its food, was almost full with produce from the garden. The woodpile was big enough to get them through the winter. The hay had grown well. There was plenty to feed the animals. Ellie fell asleep thinking of it all.

Patience was just about to drift off herself when she heard a loud pop from the fire. A few seconds later, the sound of crackling made her sit up. She jumped out of bed and ran into the main room of the cabin. Flames were sweeping across one wall and ready to leap to the next.

"Fire!" she shouted. "Fire!" Black smoke was filling the room. Patience shook the children awake and rushed them to the door. There wasn't time to save anything but themselves.

"The chest!" shouted Ellie. "I've got to get it."

"No!" yelled Patience. "Go! Get out!" She shoved Ellie through the door into the cold night air. The light from the full moon washed across Ellie's face. She was sobbing.

Patience made a decision. She dropped to the floor of the cabin and crawled to where the chest sat. Flames had not yet reached that corner of the room. Patience wasn't sure where her strength came from that night, but she stood up and hoisted the chest from the floor. She turned and dashed for the door.

Just as Patience made it out, the roof crashed in behind her. Sparks and flames shot into the air. The cabin, and everything in it, disappeared before the Doaks' eyes. There was no one for miles around to call for help.

That night they slept in the barn, huddled together under the hay for warmth. Ellie was the first to wake, confused. A piece of hay was tickling her nose. Where was she? Suddenly she knew. She rushed out of the barn to check on the cabin. Except for a few charred bits of wood, it was gone.

But there, a few feet beyond where the door had been, sat the chest. Covered with dew, it sparkled in the morning sunlight. Then Ellie remembered: Patience had saved it for her. She opened the lid now and examined the things inside. They were all there: Ruby's picture, her diary, her dress. Ellie felt a flood of thankfulness.

Cabins can be replaced, she thought. *The memories of Ma can't be.*

The Doaks would have to start all over. They'd have to replace everything—clothes, furniture, and kitchen tools. But they could make do. They always had, and Ellie knew just where to begin.

She unfolded the old wedding dress and shook it out. Made from soft wool, it was exactly the right size for Patience. Ellie carried it into the barn. Patience was just beginning to stir from her sleep. Ellie laid the dress on the hay next to her.

"Everything's gone," said Ellie. "But here's a dress you can wear today. We'll get things figured out."

Frontier Life

For many families settling the frontier, life was difficult. They had traveled great distances to reach the West and left many comforts behind them. Home on the frontier might be a tar paper shack that was freezing in the winter and stifling hot in the summer. Some settlers lived in sod houses with dirt floors that became muddy when it rained. In the late 1880s, droughts in places like South Dakota made it very difficult for settlers to grow crops.

There was always work to be done on a homestead. There were fields to plow, animals to feed, fuel to gather, and water to carry. Children helped with all these tasks.

Despite the hardships, many settlers refused to give up their dreams. Through hard work, they prospered. Here are the words of Elinore Pruitt Stewart, a homesteader in Wyoming: "Any woman who can stand her own company, can see the beauty of the sunset, loves growing things, and is willing to put in as much time at careful labor as she does over the washtub, will certainly succeed; will have independence, plenty to eat all the time, and a home of her own in the end."